A CAB AT THE DOOR

A CAB
AT THE DOOR

An Autobiography: Early Years

V. S. PRITCHETT

READERS UNION
CHATTO & WINDUS
LONDON 1968

This RU edition was produced in 1968 for sale to its members only by
Readers Union Limited, 10-13 Bedford Street, London W.C.2 and at
Letchworth Garden City, Herts. Full details of membership may be
obtained from our London address.

Originally published by Chatto and Windus Ltd. Reprinted for Readers
Union by Hollen Street Press Ltd, Slough.

To Dorothy

Chapter 1

IN our family, as far as we are concerned, we were born and what happened before that is myth. Go back two generations and the names and lives of our forbears vanish into the common grass. All we could get out of mother was that her grandfather had once taken a horse to Dublin; and sometimes in my father's expansive histories, *his* grandfather had owned trawlers in Hull, but when an abashed regard for fact, uncommon in my father, touched him in his eighties, he told us that this ancestor, a decayed seaman, was last seen gutting herrings at a bench in the fishmarket of that city. The only certainty is that I come from a set of story tellers and moralists and that neither party cared much for the precise. The story tellers were for ever changing the tale and the moralists tampering with it in order to put it in an edifying light. On my mother's side they were all pagans, and she a rootless London pagan, a fog-worshipper, brought up on the folk-lore of the North London streets; on my father's side they were harsh, lonely, God-ridden sea or country people who had been settled along the Yorkshire coasts or among its moors and fells for hundreds of years. There is enough in the differences between North and South to explain the battles and uncertainties of a lifetime. "How I got into you lot, I don't know", my mother used to say on and off all her life, looking at us with fear, as if my father and not herself had given birth to us. She was there, she conveyed, because she had been captured. It made her unbelieving and sly.

A good many shots must have been fired during the courtship of my parents and many more when I was born in lodgings over a toy shop in the middle of Ipswich at the end of 1900. Why Ipswich? My parents had no connection with the town. The moment could not have been worse. Queen Victoria was dying and my mother, young and cheerful though she was, identified herself, as the decent London poor do, with all the females of the Royal Family, especially with their pregnancies and funerals. She was a natural Victorian; the past with all its sadness meant more to her than the hopes of the new century. I was to be called Victoria, but now surgery had to be done on the name, and quickly too, for my father's father, a Congregationalist Minister in Repton, was pressing for me to be called Marcus Aurelius. The real trouble was more serious.

On my birth certificate my father's trade is written "Stationer (master)". An ambitious young man, he had given up his job as a shop assistant in Kentish Town and had opened a small newsagents and stationers in the Rushmere district of Ipswich. He did not know the city and had gone there because he thought he had a superb "opening". He did not know the trade but he had found "premises"—a word that was sacramental to him all his life. He spoke of "premises" as others speak of the New Jerusalem. He had no capital. He was only twenty-two; the venture was modest, almost pastoral; but he had smelled the Edwardian boom and it enlarged a flaw that had—I have been told—even then become noticeable in his character. One of nature's salesmen, he was even more one of nature's buyers. He looked at the measly little shop, stripped it and put in counters, cabinets and shelves ("You know your father, dear"). The suspicious Suffolk folk hated this modern splash and saw that he had spent so much on fittings that he had nothing left for stock. The bright little shop stood out as a warning to all in a crafty neighbourhood. Few customers came. The new paint smelled of sin to them. At the age of twenty-two my young father was affronted and flabbergasted to find after a few months that he was bankrupt, or if not legally bankrupt, penniless and pursued.

There is a picture of him a year or two before this time. He is thin, jaunty, with thick oily black hair, a waxed moustache, and eyes caught between a hard, brash stare and a twinkle.